Same and Different

COMPARISON RHYMES

Please visit our web site at: www.garethstevens.com
For a free color catalog describing Gareth Stevens Publishing's
list of high-quality books and multimedia programs, call
1-800-542-2595 (USA) or 1-800-387-3178 (Canada).
Gareth Stevens Publishing's fax: (414) 332-3567.

Library of Congress Cataloging-in-Publication Data available upon request from publisher.
Fax (414) 336-0157 for the attention of the Publishing Records Department.

ISBN 0-8368-4097-6

First published in 2004 by
Gareth Stevens Publishing
A World Almanac Education Group Company
330 West Olive Street, Suite 100
Milwaukee, Wisconsin 53212 USA

Gareth Stevens series editor: Dorothy L. Gibbs
Gareth Stevens graphic designer: Kami M. Koenig

Printed in the United States of America

1 2 3 4 5 6 7 8 9 08 07 06 05 04

Rhyme ⏱ Time
Learning

Same and Different

COMPARISON RHYMES

by Mary Packard • illustrations by Susan Banta

Gareth Stevens Publishing
A WORLD ALMANAC EDUCATION GROUP COMPANY

"Come in, now, my little lambs.
It's much too hot out in the sun."
But Mama's lambs still want to play.
They are having so much fun.

Which playmates are little lambs?

See the people in the city.
They take taxis everywhere.
When Alexander takes a taxi,
Mama lets him pay the fare.

Which vehicles are taxis?

This store's shelves are full of toys,
Some too high to reach.
If Randy didn't have to choose,
He'd take home one of each!

Which truck does not look
like the others?

Bunny's skating on the pond
With little sister Kate.
He's going to show her how to do
A perfect figure eight.

Which skaters are bunnies?

8

Six little pigs are dancing.
See them smile and point their toes?
They remember every pirouette.
They've practiced — and it shows!

Which dancers'
shoes don't match?

Max looks in the window
Of his favorite candy store.
Today, he'd like a lollipop —
Or, maybe, three or four.

Which lollipops are the same?

Barney's buying flowers
To make a nice bouquet.
He'll give it to his mother
To brighten up her day.

Which flowers
are red?

It's circus time. Come one! Come all!
See lots of silly clowns.
Some of them look happy,
And some wear droopy frowns.

Which clowns have
red noses?

It's fun to climb. It's fun to slide.
It's so much fun to swing.
A playground is the perfect place
To do most everything.

Which animals are
wearing blue mittens?

The squirrels up in the attic
Love Grandma's fancy clothes.
They dress up in her shoes
     and hats,
But Grandma never knows.

Which squirrels are
wearing high-heeled shoes?

Kittens in hot-air balloons
Above the clouds so high
Couldn't have a better way
To float across the sky.

Which hot-air balloons
look the same?

To Parents and Teachers:

Playing "same and different" games can help children sharpen their observation skills, and you can play these games almost anywhere. At a supermarket, for example, you could ask a child to name all the vegetables that are not green. On the street, you might have the child point out cars that are the same color. Use the pictures below to start playing a "same and different" game.

Which dancing pig is dressed differently?

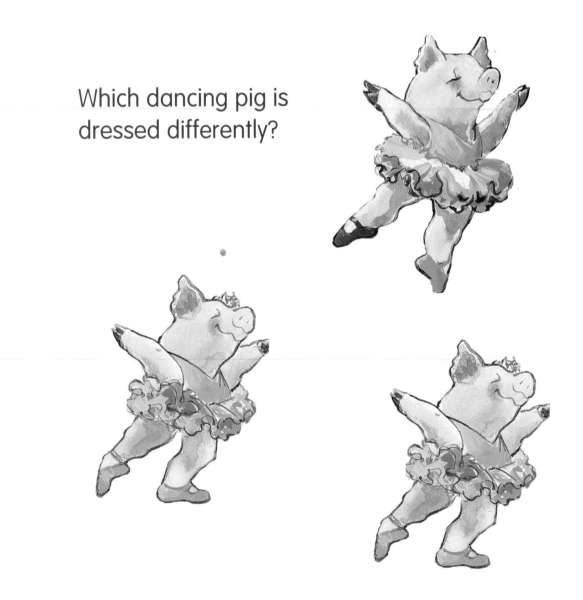